Asia-Europe Meeting

20 YEARS OF ASIA-EUROPE RELATIONS

Co-published by

Asia-Europe Foundation (ASEF)
31 Heng Mui Keng Terrace, Singapore 119595
and

World Scientific Publishing Co. Pte. Ltd.
5 Toh Tuck Link, Singapore 596224
USA office: 27 Warren Street, Suite 401-402, Hackensack, NJ 07601
UK office: 57 Shelton Street, Covent Garden, London WC2H 9HE

ASEF Team: Debasmita Dasgupta, Rafael Secades, R. Raj Kumar

Library of Congress Cataloging-in-Publication Data
Names: Kek, Peggy, editor. | Container of (work): Goh, Chok Tong, 1941–
    Asia-Europe Meeting (ASEM), a bridge between East and West. |
    Asia-Europe Meeting, honouree.
Title: 20 years of Asia-Europe relations / [edited by] Peggy Kek.
Description: New Jersey : World Scientific, [2016] | Includes bibliographical references and index.
Identifiers: LCCN 2016015757| ISBN 9789813140233 (hardcover) |
    ISBN 9789813140240 (softcover)
Subjects: LCSH: Asia-Europe Meeting. | Asia--Foreign relations--Europe. |
    Europe--Foreign relations--Asia.
Classification: LCC DS33.4.E85 C45 2016 | DDC 327.504--dc23
LC record available at https://lccn.loc.gov/2016015757

British Library Cataloguing-in-Publication Data
A catalogue record for this book is available from the British Library.

Desk Editors: Dong Lixi/Jiang Yulin
Artists: Jimmy Low/Loo Chuan Ming

Asia-Europe Meeting

20 YEARS OF
ASIA-EUROPE
RELATIONS

Editor

Peggy Kek

ASIA-EUROPE
FOUNDATION

World Scientific
www.worldscientific.com

Asia-Europe Meeting

About Asia-Europe Meeting (ASEM)

The Asia-Europe Meeting (ASEM) is an intergovernmental forum for dialogue and cooperation established in 1996 to deepen relations between Asia and Europe, which addresses political, economic and socio-cultural issues of common concern.

ASEM brings together 53 partners: Australia, Austria, Bangladesh, Belgium, Brunei Darussalam, Bulgaria, Cambodia, China, Croatia, Cyprus, the Czech Republic, Denmark, Estonia, Finland, France, Germany, Greece, Hungary, India, Indonesia, Ireland, Italy, Japan, Kazakhstan, Korea, the Lao PDR, Latvia, Lithuania, Luxembourg, Malaysia, Malta, Mongolia, Myanmar, the Netherlands, New Zealand, Norway, Pakistan, the Philippines, Poland, Portugal, Romania, the Russian Federation, Singapore, Slovakia, Slovenia, Spain, Sweden, Switzerland, Thailand, the United Kingdom, and Viet Nam plus the ASEAN Secretariat and the European Union.

For more information, please visit **www.aseminfoboard.org**

ASIA-EUROPE FOUNDATION

About Asia-Europe Foundation (ASEF)

The Asia-Europe Foundation (ASEF) promotes understanding, strengthens relationships and facilitates cooperation among the people, institutions and organisations of Asia and Europe. ASEF enhances dialogue, enables exchanges and encourages collaboration across the thematic areas of culture, economy, education, governance, public health and sustainable development.

ASEF is an intergovernmental not-for-profit organisation located in Singapore. Founded in 1997, it is the only institution of the Asia-Europe Meeting (ASEM).

Together with about 750 partner organisations ASEF has run more than 700 projects, mainly conferences, seminars and workshops. Over 20,000 Asians and Europeans have actively participated in its activities and it has reached much wider audiences through its networks, web-portals, publications, exhibitions and lectures.

For more information, please visit **www.asef.org**

ASEM Summits in Pictures

1st Asia-Europe Meeting Summit (ASEM1)
Bangkok, Thailand, 1996

2nd Asia-Europe Meeting Summit (ASEM2)
London, United Kingdom, 1998

3rd Asia-Europe Meeting Summit (ASEM3)
Seoul, South Korea, 2000

4th Asia-Europe Meeting Summit (ASEM4)
Copenhagen, Denmark, 2002

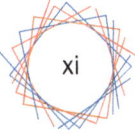

5th Asia-Europe Meeting Summit (ASEM5)
Hanoi, Viet Nam, 2004

6th Asia-Europe Meeting Summit (ASEM6)
Helsinki, Finland, 2006

7th Asia-Europe Meeting Summit (ASEM7)
Beijing, China, 2008

8th Asia-Europe Meeting Summit (ASEM8)
Brussels, Belgium, 2010

9th Asia-Europe Meeting Summit (ASEM9)
Vientiane, Lao PDR, 2012

10th Asia-Europe Meeting Summit (ASEM10)
Milan, Italy, 2014

Contents

ASEM: THE FUTURE, BUILDING ON THE PAST AND PRESENT

xx

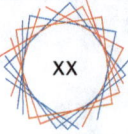

Foreword

by **Ambassador ZHANG Yan**
Executive Director
Asia-Europe Foundation (ASEF)

2016 marks the 20th Anniversary of the Asia-Europe Meeting (ASEM) process. Since the 1st ASEM Summit (ASEM1) held on 1 March 1996 in Bangkok, Thailand, ASEM has evolved into an important forum for high-level political dialogue, aiming at enhancing Asia-Europe relations and promoting interactions and cooperation between the peoples of both regions. Starting with 26 founding partners, ASEM has grown to a bi-regional node today connecting 53 partners, which manifests the vitality and potential of the ASEM process, as well as its appeal to Asian and European countries. Without doubt, the ASEM process has played and will continue to play an irreplaceable role in the efforts to promote peace, stability and prosperity of both Asia and Europe. As the ASEM process ushers in the third decade, it needs to adapt to fast-changing

international and regional situations, in order to meet multi-faceted challenges and the high expectations of ASEM partners. In July 2016, the 11th ASEM Summit (ASEM11) will take place in Ulaanbaatar, Mongolia, the outcome of which will represent another milestone in the history of the ASEM process.

The Asia-Europe Foundation (ASEF) is the only institution set up by ASEM partners in 1997, with a mandate to promote exchanges and strengthen mutual understanding between the peoples of Asia and Europe. To contribute to the commemoration of ASEM's 20th Anniversary and to add value to the success of ASEM11, ASEF has taken the initiative to present this special publication entitled *"20 Years of Asia-Europe Relations"*. The book is a collection of essays contributed by eminent political figures and government representatives from ASEM partners, reflecting on ASEM's evolution over the past two decades as well as looking into its future development.

I am grateful to all the authors who have spared precious time to share their insights and perspectives about the past, present and future of the ASEM process and the evolution of the Asia-Europe relations. I hope that these essays will help readers understand ASEM better, and learn more about its achievements and strengths, as well as the challenges ahead. I also hope that this publication will enhance the visibility of ASEM among the public, drawing their attention to, support for and participation in this dynamic process.

The past 20 years have been certainly a success for ASEM. Looking ahead, I wish for many more years of success to come!

Introduction: ASEM at 20

by **Peggy KEK**
Former Director of Public Affairs
Asia-Europe Foundation (ASEF)

The Asia-Europe Meeting (ASEM), established in 1996 to deepen relations between the two regions, is an intergovernmental forum, which addresses political, economic and socio-cultural issues of common concern through dialogue and cooperation. The following year, ASEM launched the Asia-Europe Foundation (ASEF) in Singapore to promote greater mutual understanding between Asia and Europe through intellectual, cultural and people-to-people exchanges.

ASEM began with 26 founding partners and over a period of 20 years, gradually expanded its partnership to 53 today. Keeping the forum nimble, ASEF remains the only formal institution founded by the grouping after two decades.

ASEF has produced this book to commemorate the 20th

Anniversary of ASEM, reflecting on its journey over the last two decades and looking forward to its future.

The first section of the book, **ASEM: New Beginnings**, contains two articles. In the opening essay, Mr GOH Chok Tong, Former Prime Minister of Singapore, a founding partner of ASEM, explains how his vision for a new "tri-polar world" grew out of the end of the Cold War in the early 1990s. This vision underpins the impetus for the launch of ASEM, a proposal for a new "institutional link to complete the triangle" through closer relations between Asia and Europe to complement the close ties that America already had with the two regions.

The opening essay is followed by an article from Mongolia, which joined ASEM in 2008 and is the host of the 11th ASEM Summit (ASEM11) in 2016 that begins a new decade of engagement for the two regions. Prime Minister of Mongolia, Mr Chimediin SAIKHANBILEG, points to the enlarged partnership of ASEM as an indication of its continuing relevance and highlights the usefulness of its unique "informality and openness to free exchange of views".

The second section of the book, **ASEM: The Future, Building on the Past and Present**, contains essays that express partners' appreciation for what ASEM has achieved over the last two decades and their aspirations for its future. The essays are arranged in alphabetical order by country.

Several essays in this section mention "connectivity". ZENG Peiyan, President of the China Center for International Economic Exchanges (CCIEE), posits that connectivity should include a "vibrant and open connectivity network that pools talent and resources from all stakeholders".

German Federal Minister of Foreign Affairs, Frank-Walter STEINMEIER reflects on the evolution of ASEM, noting changes in the membership and the introduction of new themes into the forum over the years. Looking forward, he observes that "connectivity is the name of the game" and believes that "the challenge for the 21st century statecraft will be to devise joint solutions for global issues".

Indonesian Minister of Education and Culture, Anies BASWEDAN, focuses on education, sharing his country's experiences in raising enrolment rates and pushing lifelong learning for better employment prospects.

Former Prime Minister of Italy, Romano PRODI, who was also the President of the European Commission in ASEM's nascent years, urges ASEM to "invest its institutional capabilities and diplomatic skills" in the New Silk Road project. He welcomes the establishment of the Asian Infrastructure Investment Bank too, noting that successful financing of infrastructure projects could help "rising economies" to emerge as "new poles of growth".

Foreign Minister for Japan, Fumio KISHIDA, advocates tourism as a field, which could increase connectivity but also points out the risks of increased cross-border connectivity such as the spread of infectious diseases.

Kazakhstan joined ASEM in 2014 and is one of the newest ASEM partners. Foreign Minister Erlan IDRISSOV spells out the areas in which he believes his country can contribute to the ASEM dialogue, including economic cooperation, global climate change and nuclear energy.

KIM Jongdeok, Minister of Culture, Sports and Tourism of the Republic of Korea, underlines the role of cultural understanding not just in adding value to the economy through creative industries but also in building measures and partnerships to help prevent terror attacks.

Luxembourg's Minister for Foreign and European Affairs, Jean ASSELBORN, believes that connectivity will be "the key feature of ASEM's third decade". Observing that connectivity "has so far mostly been dealt within regional organisations or at national levels", he suggests that ASEM could "create specific-added-value" by working across regions.

Jet BUSSEMAKER, Minister of Education, Culture and Science of the Netherlands, makes the case that our economies are "becoming more cultural in nature and that the economic and social significance of creativity" is growing.

In her commentary, she stresses the need to revisit the areas of financing and education to support the creative industries.

The section is rounded out by an article from Margot WALLSTRÖM, Swedish Minister for Foreign Affairs. Recalling the inaugural ASEM Informal Seminar on Human Rights launched by Sweden and France in 1997, she notes many improvements in the world since then. However, she thinks that "the world has again become more unpredictable and less secure" and believes that "the involvement of women is imperative to ensure peace and security". She is confident of continued commitment to the seminar series which is now in its 15th edition.

Many of the writers refer to events organised by ASEF, and it is a resounding endorsement for the only permanent institution set up by ASEM. The third section of the book, entitled **ASEM and ASEF**, comprises an article written by two management staff from the very first team of ASEF. Ambassador Tommy KOH was the founding Executive Director and I was the first Director of Public Affairs. We reflect on the challenges and opportunities of ASEF then and now and urge the extended ASEM family to put their weight fully behind the organisation.

This collection of essays provides insights into a range of themes from economics to education, culture to climate change, and is a true reflection of the breadth and depth of issues that

engage ASEM partners. The usefulness of the ASEM process as a forum for dialogue and platform for collaboration comes through clearly. The essays provide not only reflections on the history of ASEM but also expressions of hope for its future on the eve of its 21st year.

ASEM: NEW BEGINNINGS

The Asia-Europe Meeting (ASEM): A Bridge between East and West

by **GOH Chok Tong**
Former Prime Minister
Singapore

When I became Prime Minister of Singapore in 1990, the Cold War had ended and the world was transiting to a new order. Asia was experiencing a period of unprecedented high economic growth: Japan and the so-called "Asian Tigers" – Hong Kong, Singapore, South Korea and Taiwan – led this wave, followed by the re-emergence of China and India. In Europe, the entry into force of the Maastricht Treaty on 1 November 1993 laid a firm foundation for closer economic and financial integration. With the collapse of the Soviet Union and the ascendency of North America, East Asia and Western Europe, a tri-polar world order was taking shape.

I was of the view that if we could connect these three economic blocs together like a triangle, the result would be a more stable geopolitical environment for all. North America and Europe already had longstanding institutional linkages, by virtue of their shared history and culture. North America and East Asia had also begun to forge closer ties under the aegis of the Asia-Pacific Economic Cooperation (APEC). However, the missing institutional link that was needed to complete the triangle was closer relations between Asia and Europe.

Europe's interest in Asia had dwindled after the withdrawals of France from Indochina and of the UK from territories east of the Suez in the last century. On Asia's part, colonisation had dampened its enthusiasm for closer relations with Europe. Partly because of this, Western Europe was trading and investing less in Asia than in the US. In 1994, North America accounted for 25% of the European Union's (EU) total trade volume, whereas its total trade with 10 countries in East Asia (Brunei, Indonesia, Malaysia, the Philippines, Singapore, Thailand, Viet Nam, China, Japan and South Korea) made up only 8% of the total.

The World Economic Forum (WEF) Europe/East Asia Summit held in Singapore in October 1994 provided an occasion for me to seed the idea of closer dialogue between Asia and Europe at the leaders' level. European leaders then had limited contacts with a China which was not yet fully opened to foreign investments and imports. In its July 1994 Communique, "Towards a New Asia Strategy", the European Commission sought to "accord Asia a higher priority than is at present the case" and to "strengthen its economic presence in Asia in order to maintain its leading role in the world economy". Similarly, Asia wanted Europe's investments and access to its markets. Given Singapore's close relations with Association of Southeast Asian Nations (ASEAN), China and the rest of the Asia-Pacific as well as with Europe, I thought that we were well-placed to seed the idea of an Asia-Europe Meeting (ASEM).

During my official visit to France in October 1994, I proposed to Prime Minister Edouard BALLADUR the idea of establishing a regular summit for leaders from Europe and Asia to meet, to get to know each other and to develop ties between the two regions. He was receptive. The French were due to assume the EU Presidency in January 1995. Prime Minister BALLADUR undertook to sell the idea to the EU member states, and I, in turn, did likewise with Asian leaders. I secured the ASEAN leaders' support for ASEM a month later on the sidelines of the APEC summit in Bogor, Indonesia. Later, we secured China, Japan and South Korea's buy-in. On their part, the French delivered their side of the bargain. The inaugural ASEM summit was launched with great success in Bangkok in March 1996. Fifteen countries from Europe and 10 countries from Asia participated. The European Commission was also present. Our discussions were candid, fresh, free-flowing and productive. The informal nature of the dialogue allowed leaders to establish a high level of comfort and familiarity with one another. It proved to be one of ASEM's abiding strengths.

ASEM – vision and reality

This proved fortuitous as ASEM was tested very early after its birth, when Asia was hit badly by the Asian Financial Crisis in 1997. At the second ASEM summit in London in 1998, Europe sought to understand the genesis of the Asian Financial Crisis and showed concern and continued interest in its Asian partners. Our European partners demonstrated their commitment to Asia and the ASEM process by establishing the ASEM Trust Fund at this summit. It was a show of faith.

As the EU took on new members, ASEM's membership inevitably expanded. The cosiness of the early summits was lost. ASEM came under severe criticism for the lack of focus and substance. Interventions became increasingly scripted and mundane, and several ASEM summits showed poor attendance. But I think this diffusion of ASEM's focus was only one part of the story. A more important reason was the increased direct contact between European and Chinese leaders after China lifted its bamboo curtain. ASEM as a meeting venue for them had lost its salience. Another reason was the preoccupation of European leaders with more pressing domestic and EU problems. ASEM cohesion was also tested when Myanmar's application to join ASEM was blocked by the European partners. Both sides locked horns on this for a while. It was finally resolved with the admission of Myanmar in 2004.

We should not lose faith in the founding vision and value of ASEM. As the meeting point of a resurgent Asia and institutionally important Europe, Asian and European leaders continue to see ASEM's long-term strategic value. I am therefore confident that ASEM will continue to remain relevant.

Since its founding, ASEM's operating environment has been fundamentally altered by the Asian renaissance, the Eurozone crisis and recently, the global war on terror. Whatever else may change, ASEM's *raison d'être* of strengthening Asia-Europe links remains. Trade agreements such as the Trans-Pacific Partnership (TPP) and the Transatlantic Trade and Investment Partnership (TTIP), once in force, will propel the economic ties between Asia and the US, and Europe and the US respectively. But there is no similar initiative between Asia and Europe yet. ASEM therefore holds the key to realising an Asia-Europe answer to the TPP and TTIP.

ASEM should also tap on the diverse civilisational strengths of Asia and Europe to address global challenges, such as climate change, nuclear non-proliferation, and the rise of radical Islam, which uses terror, violence and killings to advance its cause. The diversity of input can only add to a more nuanced understanding of the issues and the perspectives of different countries. This in turn will enhance the resilience of individual ASEM partners to these challenges.

These are major undertakings that will occupy not only the current generation of leaders, but also future generations. Yet, leaders are not permanent members of ASEM; only their countries are. All the more cause then, for a forum like ASEM, for old, new and future leaders to continually develop their ties and understanding of each region's challenges and aspirations.

Our interactions over the last two decades have laid a strong tradition for this process to continue. ASEM has thrived as a dialogue forum because of its informality and flexibility. I think that we should not seek to transform ASEM into a more structured and bureaucratic body. Given its large size and diverse membership, ASEM's objectives are best served by fostering collegial dialogue and a genuine desire for cooperation. ASEM should continue to be viewed as a process.

The next lap

Singapore is deeply committed to the ASEM process and will contribute its energy and ideas to ensure that ASEM remains credible and effective. Singapore will also continue to support the Asia-Europe Foundation (ASEF)[1] in its mission to

---

[1] www.asef.org

strengthen people-to-people ties, and cultural and academic exchanges between the two regions.

As ASEM sets to commemorate its 20th Anniversary in 2016, its future looks bright. ASEM continues to attract new members – Croatia and Kazakhstan were admitted into ASEM in 2014, bringing ASEM's total membership to 53. Turkey and Ukraine have also started their applications. These facts are a testament to ASEM's continued value. Indeed, ASEM has effectively become a commonwealth of nations from Europe and Asia!

As a community of Asian and European nations, I believe that there is much untapped potential in ASEM. We should continue to strengthen our side of the triangle. In the words of Rudyard Kipling, *"there is neither East nor West, Border, nor Breed, nor Birth, When two strong men stand face to face, tho' they come from the ends of the earth"*. Europe and Asia must celebrate differences even as they explore common grounds. As the EU and Asia continue to deepen their respective regional integration, they should also look beyond their immediate region and create synergistic opportunities. Such habits of cooperation have only positives and no negatives. They will reinforce the peace and prosperity that our people need to lead a rich, balanced and fulfilling life.

Building on 20 Years of ASEM: Expanding Connectivity and Inclusion

by **Chimediin SAIKHANBILEG**
Prime Minister
Mongolia

The 20th Anniversary of the Asia-Europe Meeting (ASEM) is a fitting opportunity to reflect both on its past, present and future as well as on the evolving connectivity between Asia and Europe, the world's two ancient cradles of civilisations that have contributed greatly to humanity's development and prosperity.

ASEM's coming into being was a natural response to the dramatic changes in the global political and economic landscape in the mid-1990s following the end of the Cold War, at a time when Asia was emerging as a world economic powerhouse. ASEM with its distinct signature was an outcome consistent with the time.

Twenty years is a short span of time in human history, and yet the global and regional settings today are already

fundamentally different from what they were two decades ago. In spite of the challenges of rapid change, ASEM has withstood the test of time. Partly to the credit of ASEM dialogue and initiatives, Asia and Europe today enjoy much wider connectivity and greater engagement than 20 years ago.

Aspiring to make her own contribution to Asia-Europe engagement and to be a part of this multifaceted dialogue process, Mongolia joined ASEM in 2008. As Prime Minister of Mongolia and Head of the National Preparatory Council for the 2016 ASEM Summit in Ulaanbaatar, with great pride and responsibility, I am happy to inform that Mongolia is diligently preparing for this grand event. I take this opportunity to convey our sincere gratitude to the Asia-Europe Foundation (ASEF) and all ASEM partners who have been rendering valuable support and assistance in the summit preparations.

The term, *connectivity,* has become a buzzword within ASEM and Mongolia approaches the concept in its broadest sense. Mongolia, both historically and geographically, has been a bridge between Asia and Europe and strives to play a role in both "hard" and "soft" connectivity. My government seeks to further develop and expand Mongolia's existing infrastructure links between the two continents and concrete projects are being implemented in this field.

The international fora that exist for meetings and

negotiations are spacious and vast, yet it seems that there are few platforms, like ASEM, which are not burdened with rigid and complex rules of procedures or protocol regulations and allow for informal dialogue. ASEM's informality and openness to the free exchange of views are the very features that distinguish it from among other international venues. ASEM is not a negotiating body and it should be preserved as a platform for informal dialogue and exchange. We could also work towards actively using the retreat format which has proved to be so valuable.

On the eve of its 20th Anniversary a number of recommendations and advice on ASEM's future are being voiced. We find particularly valuable and thought-provoking the conclusions of the study on the future of ASEM, Symposium of the Future Direction of ASEM held in Bangkok and the Conference on the Challenge of Connectivity. We are also aware of the criticism concerning ASEM meetings. As we prepare for the summit we will take into account the merit of this criticism. We support the idea of engaging the Asian and European business communities, civil societies, youth and academia more actively into the ASEM process so as to make it more productive and result-oriented. These recommendations and conclusions are built on ASEM's 20 years of experience. In this conjunction, I would like to commend ASEF for its role in the ASEM process and as a guardian of "collective memory".

Mongolia's view is that the ASEM dialogue should continue to build on political, economic and socio-cultural pillars. We firmly believe that trade and investment, and the robust role played by the private sector are crucial for Asia-Europe economic connectivity. Twenty five years ago, Mongolia embarked on the path of free market economy and political democracy. We are fully aware of the potential that the business community can bring into trade and investment between the two continents.

Further development and advancement of tangible areas of cooperation, which now cover 17 concrete fields, should help ASEM to become more result-oriented. Mongolia is a partner in a number of these tangible areas of cooperation and has successfully organised a Seminar on Renewable Energy in Ulaanbaatar in the spring of 2015.

As I mentioned earlier the development of infrastructure connecting Asia and Europe through Mongolia is of great interest for us and we highly value the results of the 3rd ASEM Transport Ministers' Meeting (ASEM TMM3)[1] held in Riga as well as the Industry Dialogue on Connectivity held in Chongqing, China, in May 2015.

The Asia-Europe Cooperation Framework 2000 document highlights "... respect for democracy, rule of law, equality, justice and human rights ..."

---

[1] www.aseminfoboard.org/events/3rd-asem-transport-ministers-meeting-asem-tmm3

among others in its Vision into the 21st Century. These common human values are essential fundamentals for building an environment conducive to sustainable development, as we Mongols have experienced in our development efforts. On the basis of mutual respect ASEM should include these issues on its agenda.

That ASEM's ranks have doubled since its inception is a straightforward testimony to its relevance. There are more countries interested in taking up membership. Mongolia believes that in order to make Asia-Europe dialogue even more inclusive ASEM should continue to expand to include new partners.

I am confident that based on the experience we gained through hard work in the past 20 years and having matured through the test of time, the ASEM process will achieve even more success in the years to come. It is a noble duty and a matter of profound pride for Mongolia to serve for the prosperity of the peoples of Asia and Europe, and rest assured, Mongolia stands fully committed to most meaningfully advance this very responsible mission.

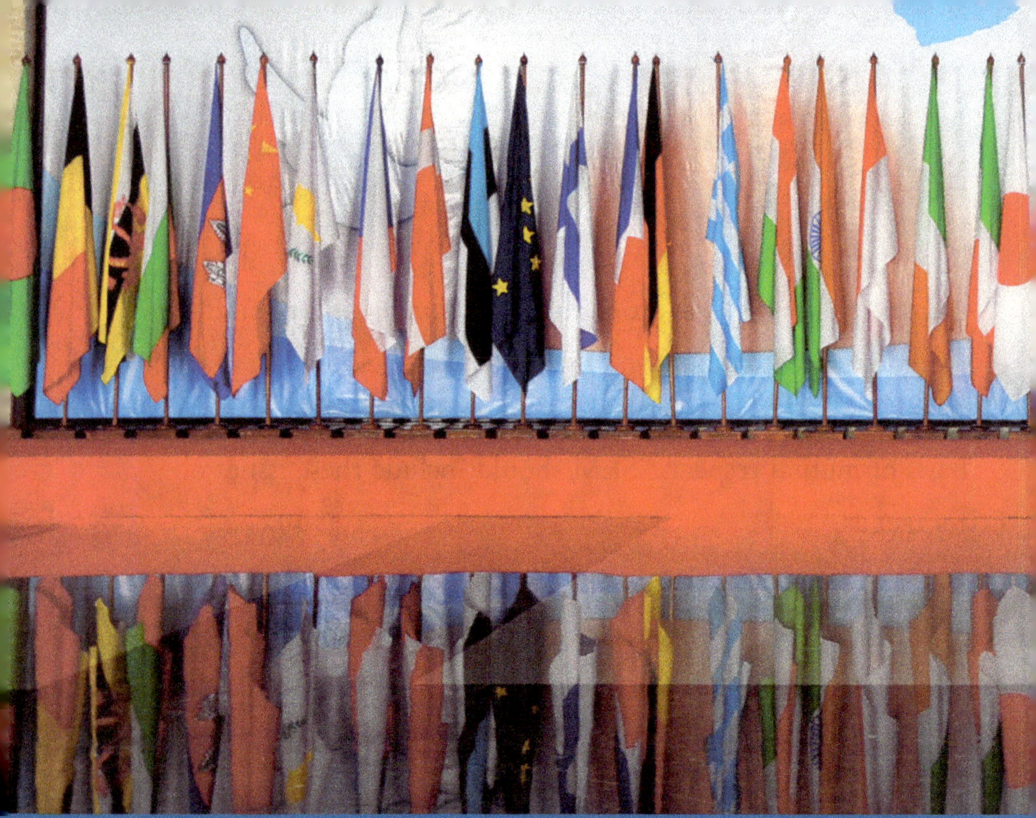

ASEM: THE FUTURE, BUILDING ON THE PAST AND PRESENT

Connectivity: Shaping the Future of ASEM

by **ZENG Peiyan**
President of China Center for International Economic
Exchanges (CCIEE)
China

The global economy has experienced intricate and volatile developments in recent years. The economic growth forecasts have been repeatedly downgraded and the growth rate of world trade is dropping sharply. Developed economies are on a weak recovery and still fraught with destabilising factors such as the debt crisis and population ageing. The growth of emerging economies slowed significantly while economic and financial risks are piling up. In a time of post-crisis, the world economy risks the possibility of entering into a "new normal" of prolonged low-speed growth. All countries are faced with the urgent task of finding new paths to sustain growth and withstand risks. Against such a background, connectivity has become the new focus of both Asian and European countries.

The Eurasian continent, as one of the pioneers of continental connectivity, opened up the Silk Road 2,000 years ago. With the deepening of globalisation and informatisation, countries around the world have become more integrated with each other than ever. Asia and Europe are neighbouring continents with high economic complementarity and extensive trade ties. The two continents are faced with common challenges of propelling structural reform and realising economic recovery. Enhancing Asia-Europe connectivity is not only a natural choice for regional cooperation and economic integration, but also a strategic initiative for promoting economic vitality and strengthening development momentum, in view of both future and practical needs. As Chinese President XI Jinping pointed out, "The connectivity we talk about today is not merely about building roads and bridges or making linear connections of different places on surface. More importantly, it should be a three-way combination of infrastructure, institutions and people-to-people exchanges and a five-way progress in policy communication, infrastructure connectivity, trade link, capital flow, and understanding among peoples. It is a wide-ranging, multi-dimensional, vibrant and open connectivity network that pools talent and resources from all stakeholders."

At the same time, a number of issues in Asia-Europe cooperation need to be addressed. A pressing one is that missing links among many countries impede economic development and cooperation. Take the China-Europe freight train for instance. Since its launch in 2015, more than 1,000 shifts have already been run. However, the cost of time and resources remains high, due to the frequent switch of trains and rails and the vast differences in customs clearance procedures. This in one way shows that Asia-Europe connectivity still faces obstacles and hindrance.

Asia is the world's most economically dynamic region while Europe is the world frontier in innovation and integration. As the interdependence among economies in the two regions is increasingly intensified, the internal need to enhance Asia-Europe connectivity grows stronger. With the large size of the economies in the two continents, their enhanced connectivity will not only strengthen regional economic vitality, but also inject new impetus to global sustainable development.

Connectivity is the necessary condition for trans-regional economic cooperation, trade, investment and personnel exchanges. Experience indicates that regional connectivity will vigorously generate positive external benefits and "1+1>2" multiplying effect. If the Eurasian continent is fully connected, the region will become the world's biggest common market which will unleash great external economic bonus for all regional countries. The promising new pattern of unified market, comprehensive industry and modern logistics will provide great opportunity for long-term common growth.

Established 20 years ago, Asia-Europe Meeting (ASEM) has developed into the main platform for dialogue and cooperation for 53 Asian and European members. Its high-level, broad representation and flexible formats have proven to be effective in pursuing common interests and promoting win-win cooperation. On the other hand, with the flourishing of new regional and trans-regional cooperation mechanisms, a loose dialogue mechanism like ASEM faces more challenges than before, especially when it lacks focus and concrete cooperation. In order to play its full role under the new circumstances and better respond to the calls of its members, there is a growing urgency for ASEM to strengthen coordination mechanisms and promote concrete cooperation.

Connectivity provides a window of opportunity to prioritise and consolidate all-round cooperation so as to fulfil the true potential of ASEM. As Mr GOH Chok Tong, one of my old friends and the former Prime Minister of Singapore said, "As the EU and Asia continue to deepen their respective regional integration, they also look beyond their immediate region and create synergistic opportunities."

The prospect of ASEM connectivity is promising. However, as a grand and systematic project, it will also be faced with various challenges, such as how to match up the complex infrastructure plans and fill the financing gaps, how to harmonise policies and regulations while meeting various development aspirations and so on. As an old Chinese saying goes, "A real man should constantly strive for self-perfection." To accomplish the systematic project of connectivity, we need all members within the region to make concerted efforts. Strategic planning, sincerity and a strong determination to build a community of shared responsibilities and destinies are core to the success of a well-connected ASEM.

ASEM members have come up with numerous ambitious development plans in recent years, such as the EU Infrastructure Investment Plan, the Master Plan on ASEAN Connectivity, the Belt and Road Initiative as well as the Asian Infrastructure Investment Bank. We are pleased to note that infrastructure connectivity has in the past few years taken the lead and produced satisfactory outcomes particularly in the areas of transportation, telecommunication and energy. Large-scale joint projects in these areas have not only tremendously fuelled local development in the short term, but will also benefit more nations and peoples in Asia and Europe in the long term.

Chinese Premier LI Keqiang pointed out at the 10th ASEM Summit[1] that "connectivity leads to prosperity". ASEM members agreed to list connectivity as a standing agenda item of ASEM

---

[1] www.aseminfoboard.org/events/10th-asem-summit-asem10

at the 12th ASEM Foreign Ministers' Meeting (ASEM FMM12) in 2015. The ASEM Industry Dialogue on Connectivity held last May in Chongqing, China, expressed strong solidarity for ASEM connectivity. These positive steps will certainly facilitate connectivity cooperation across the region.

The era of "Great Connectivity" is already at our doorstep. It is a historical process and a driving force for development. At the important juncture of the 20th Anniversary of ASEM, we should join hands to advance this process and strengthen the force for opening a new chapter of the Asia-Europe cooperation.

20 Years of Asia-Europe Meeting from 1996 to 2016: An Active Partnership – Ready for the Next Decades

by **Frank-Walter STEINMEIER**
Federal Minister for Foreign Affairs
Germany

When I think about Asia, it is the busy street-life and the modern skylines of so many vibrant Asian cities which first come to my mind. They are the most visible signs of the Asia-Pacific's steady rise and its impressive growth rates, which are also mirrored by the latest trade figures for Germany: in 2015, the German trade volume with the Asia-Pacific countries grew by 12.7% in imports alone, thereby amounting to a total trade volume of approximately 340 billion Euros. Trade between Asia and Europe is only one aspect. Connectivity is the new name of the game. This is where the Asia-Europe Meeting (ASEM) excels: ASEM stands for networking, joining, connecting — ASEM is 100% connectivity.

ASEM was founded 20 years ago to create a place for Asia and Europe to meet and share ideas, to foster mutual understanding, cooperation and confidence-building — at the highest level of heads of state and government, as well as at the expert level, where numerous best practices offer insight into the other ASEM partners' experience and knowledge. This is also true for the Asia-Europe Foundation (ASEF), ASEM's non-governmental pillar. ASEF brings together civil society from Asia and Europe, through various initiatives such as the "Asia-Europe Classroom" or the most recent "Young Leaders Summit". ASEF is helping to connect the next generations with each other, and reaching out to the ASEM decision-makers, as we witnessed at our last meeting in Luxembourg in November 2015.

Looking at ASEM over the past decades, ASEM succeeded in keeping this original "ASEM way". When I chaired the 8th ASEM Foreign Ministers' Meeting (ASEM FMM8) in Hamburg in 2007, I remember very constructive and lively discussions with my colleagues from then 45 countries on the current political issues of that time. I also recall that there were more than 60 bilateral meetings in Hamburg between foreign ministers from Asia and Europe, offering an excellent occasion to get to know each other, to sound out common ground — and also get an idea of the limits of common ground.

ASEM of today is even larger than it was in 2007, with

now a more than a doubled membership, from 26 countries in 1996 to 53 in 2016, underlining how attractive ASEM is for countries in Asia and Europe. In addition to the growing ASEM-membership, also the issues we discuss have multiplied and evolved further, thereby keeping track of the shifting challenges of today's world. This is actually one of ASEM's greatest features: always ready for change, flexible, open to new members and issues, and adapting quickly.

For example, when Germany introduced the new idea of a social dimension in ASEM with the first ASEM Ministerial Meeting for Labour and Employment (ASEM LEMC1) in Germany, our ASEM partners immediately joined in to discuss the issues of decent work, social protection, international social standards and fair trade. The very active ASEM dialogue on social issues was being sustained over the past years, with regular follow-up meetings in Indonesia, the Netherlands, Viet Nam and most recently in Bulgaria. ASEM has proven to be a transparent laboratory where ASEM partners can test ideas and concepts. If they are successful, there is follow-up; if not, then it was worth a try.

Another remarkable development in ASEM is the introduction of innovative approaches: the ASEM Transport Ministers' Meetings (ASEM TMM), initiated in Lithuania in 2009, sustained in China in 2011 and most recently in Latvia in 2015 (and to be followed-up in Indonesia in 2017), introduced a new concept: not only the ASEM-Transport Ministers gathered in Riga, but also other connectivity-stakeholders, such as the private sector, international finance institutes and scientists, actually inspired us for our current Organization for Security and Co-operation in Europe (OSCE) Chairmanship. We will invite the OSCE members as well as partners of the OSCE for a special OSCE connectivity conference in May 2016 in Germany, and build on the OSCE's asset as a geographical bridge between Asia and Europe.

Good connectivity is also needed for prosperity and growth and for building trust and stability. All these elements are essential for Asia and Europe, when we join efforts to share the responsibility to address the challenges of our times. Migration is one of these challenges. I repeat my plea that a country's true strength has to be measured by its willingness and ability to assume responsibility, also beyond its own borders. Furthermore, we are increasingly faced with new conflict structure, with eroding orders, with conflict less between states and more and more often between states and non-state actors. For that reason we need to bridge rifts and to build bridges and solid networks, also among Asian and European partners.

The current challenges in Asia-Pacific might be different ones than those in Europe. Still, Europe and Asia should continue, also within the ASEM framework, to work together for global responsibility, as a step-by-step process fostering dialogue and stability. Europe has to take Asia's views into account, and vice versa. The challenge for the 21st century statecraft will be to devise joint solutions for global issues. I trust that Asia and Europe will continue to be strong partners in this challenge and will keep ASEM as a relevant and indispensable forum in this endeavour.

With ASEM cooperation, we are not looking for front-page news. It is rather the long-term and patient weaving of ties and networks that we work on, connecting Asia and Europe in an active partnership — ready for the next decades.

H.E. Mr. Anies Baswedan
Minister of Education and Culture
Republic of Indonesia

Making Employability Work: Indonesia's Experience

by **Anies BASWEDAN**
Minister of Education and Culture
Republic of Indonesia

T he spread and spirit of democracy has encouraged people from diverse backgrounds to engage in a harmonious dialogue on a wide range of issues. The Asia-Europe Meeting (ASEM) has undertaken an important role in bringing countries from Asia and Europe together to discuss essential matters, including those in the education area. Since the 1st ASEM Meeting of Ministers for Education (ASEM ME1) held in Berlin, Germany, in 2008, significant progress has been made to address educational issues of the 21st century that particularly fall under four priorities: 1) Quality Assurance and Recognition, 2) Engaging Business and Industry in Education, 3) Balanced Mobility, and 4) Lifelong Learning including Technical Vocational Education and Training.

Throughout the ASEM Education Process, we have emphasised human and skill development for better employability. Different countries face different challenges in improving employability. Indonesia in particular faces enormous challenges due to the vast number of youths. This article aims to share Indonesia's experience and best practices in improving employability.

In 2012, the United Nations Development Programme (UNDP) released a study revealing that more than 60% of the world population is in Asia, whilst population in Europe accounts for 10% of the world's total population. The number of working-age population in Asia is projected to increase by 22% from 2.8 billion in 2010 to 3.4 billion in 2050 (Yidan Wang, World Bank, 2012). On the other hand, Europe's population rate is projected to decrease by 23% from 0.5 billion to 0.38 billion during the same period. An increased population generates increased demand and consumption for goods and services, which in turn results in a rising demand for workers. In this regard, the opportunity to fill the demand for skilful workers is open to any region or country with the most working-age population, including Indonesia.

Indonesia has the world's fourth largest population and its economy could become the seventh largest economy in the world by 2030 (McKinsey, 2013). To support the economy Indonesia will require 113 million skilled workers. This number could easily be fulfilled since the number of working age population in 2014 reached approximately 120 million (Statistics Indonesia, 2016). However, the majority of the workers have not yet acquired the desired level of skills. This situation needs to change. In trying to achieve greater productivity, there has been a steady increase in demand for skilled and high-skilled workers and a decrease in demand for unskilled and low-skilled workers. Those with lower levels of education are more likely to be unemployed whilst those with higher levels of education are more likely to be employed.

The message is clear. The urgency and necessity to devise a comprehensive policy to improve the employability of the working age population through increased education and skills is obvious. According to the Pearson Learning Curve (2014), developing countries must teach effective basic skills such as mathematics and literacy before embarking on more advanced skills (National Medium Term Development Plan 2015-2019, p. xix). Against this background, a strong focus on the quality of basic education is still required and the priority for the next five years must be directed towards the improvement of students' achievement, vocational and technical skills as well as higher education. The direction of education development in 2015-2019 covers rather ambitious but feasible targets as follow:

- Average years of schooling of the population aged over 15 years: 8.8 years
- Average literacy rate of the population aged 15 years and over: 96.1%
- Percentage of primary education accredited B or higher: 84.2%
- Percentage of junior secondary accredited B or higher: 81.6%
- Percentage of senior secondary accredited B or higher: 84.6%
- Percentage of skill competence of senior vocational accredited B or higher: 65%
- Gross Enrolment Ratio of junior secondary between 20% poorest and 20% richest population: 0.90
- Gross Enrolment Ratio of senior secondary including vocational between 20% poorest and 20% richest population: 0.60

To date, the Government of Indonesia has pledged solid commitment to the development of the education sector. For over a decade, the government has been consistently increasing education investment and reform at all levels. Government expenditure in education has tripled, resulting in the expansion of education access, particularly for the marginalised. Statistics clearly show that gross enrolment ratios of secondary and tertiary education have increased exponentially.

More initiatives have been launched to support the achievement of education targets, particularly employment-oriented education. *First*, the Universal Secondary Education program increases the compulsory period of study for school-aged children from 9 years to 12 years. *Second*, Technical and Vocational Education and Training (TVET) and lifelong learning covers the adjustment of education and employment. TVET is conducted by accelerating the development of vocational schools. Community Colleges and Polytechnics are designed to meet the local needs and national priorities, based on the Master Plan of Acceleration and Extension of Indonesia's Economic Development (MPAEIED) program. Further to that, in order to ensure better employment, a comprehensive adjustment in quantity, quality, location, and time, the Indonesian Qualification Framework (IQF) has been established to improve the quality. *Third*, establishing community colleges in each district to support the expansion of quality education in the province is mandated by Law No.22/2012 on Higher Education. Indonesia is close to achieving the target gross enrolment ratio of tertiary education of 30% or approximately 5 million of the students enrolled.

The dialogue on education with ASEM has been showing positive progress. Indonesia reiterates its strong commitment by supporting initiatives, sharing best practices and lessons learned on the development of education in Asian and European countries. To achieve the goals of the ASEM Education Process on better employability, ASEM needs to focus on the development and nurturing of the quality of education systems. Such aspects are addressed in our first priority in the ASEM Education Process, namely, Quality Assurance and Recognition. Several activities under this topic are carried out, including: a) Working Group on Mobility of Higher Education and Ensuring Quality Assurance of Higher Education among ASEAN plus Three Countries and b) Working Group Meeting for Implementing the ASEM Recognition Bridging Declaration. The quality enhancement in our education system is clearly needed at all levels. With the increase of quality, students are able to achieve better learning outcomes and acquire better knowledge.

Under the second priority, ASEM members construct collaboration between business and industry sectors and the educational system. This collaboration successfully stimulates members to jointly establish several activities such as the "ASEM Work Placement Pilot Programme" which allows students from Asia and Europe to experience the international working environment, and the "ASEM Rectors Conference and Students Forum"[1] that provides a platform for rectors and students to discuss the relationship between higher education institutions and business.

---

[1] www.asef.org/projects/programmes/529-ARC

The third priority emphasises balanced mobility, where ASEM members pay close attention to the trend of exchange of students and staff among countries in both regions. This is one common obstacle that we are currently facing. The imbalance between numbers of student and staff of Asia and those of Europe will prevent the involved actors to gain the necessary international experience and training to boost their employability.

In this regard, ASEM members are continually encouraged to extend their commitment to work together in several ASEM education activities such as "ASEM Joint Curriculum Development Project" (which allows students from Asia and Europe to experience different learning cultures and absorb best practices from different countries); "Asia-Europe Institute (AEI) – ASEM Summer Camps (AEI-ASC)" and "ASEF Summer University[2]" which provide students and staff with international experiences.

Through the fourth pillar, ASEM members are promoting lifelong learning opportunities. Lifelong learning will provide the means to develop skills and working life capabilities. Activities under this pillar include the "Working Group on Innovative Competences and Entrepreneurship Education"

---

[2] www.asef.org/projects/programmes/522-au

which allows the members to share their best practices, and analyse and evaluate innovation and entrepreneurship education.

Within the framework of ASEM cooperation, I believe that we will overcome our common obstacles by supporting one another. ASEM consists of 53 partners[3] that have different education systems, and experience different policy and education achievements. The opportunity the forum has to offer is enormous. We can learn from each other's experiences and best practices to reach a common universal goal which is to develop human capital for the advancement of each country. We have set our future plan. The next step is to start executing the plan and agenda to enrich the contribution of education to the society at large and to people-to-people contact, particularly between Asia and Europe.

---

[3]   Asia: Australia, Bangladesh, Brunei Darussalam, Cambodia, China, India, Indonesia, Japan, Kazakhstan, Korea, Laos, Malaysia, Mongolia, Myanmar, New Zealand, Pakistan, the Philippines, Russia, Singapore, Thailand, Viet Nam and ASEAN Secretariat.

Europe: Austria, Belgium, Bulgaria, Croatia, Cyprus, Czech Republic, Denmark, Estonia, Finland, France, Germany, Greece, Hungary, Ireland, Italy, Latvia, Lithuania, Luxembourg, Malta, the Netherlands, Norway, Poland, Portugal, Romania, Slovenia, Slovak Republic, Spain, Sweden, Switzerland, United Kingdom and European Union.

www.aseminfoboard.org

Bibliography

National Medium Term Development Plan 2015-2019. Jakarta: Ministry of Education and Culture, Indonesia, 2015

Wang, Yidan. *Education in a Changing World: Flexibility, Skills, and Employability.* Washington DC: The World Bank, 2012

The Beginning and Future of ASEM: The Potential of the Silk Road Project and the AIIB

by **Romano PRODI**
Former Prime Minister, Italy and
Former President, European Commission

F or almost 20 years the Asia-Europe Meeting (ASEM) has sought to deepen and foster cooperation between the Old Continent and what I believe will be one of the key regional areas of the future. The gradual enlargement of ASEM, from 26 to its current 53 members, is the strongest evidence of its success so far. And the recent inclusion of states like Norway, Switzerland, and Kazakhstan is the certitude of its lasting future.

International politics and global economics are often described as a game between states, in which international organisations play a marginal role. Today, in particular, world politics and economics are viewed as a competition and partnership between the United States and China. Although in the next decades there might be such an evolution, this is not how the world works today. The geographical, political and economic space between Europe and Asia, for example, is still of fundamental importance. The on-going crises in Ukraine and in the Middle East are evidence of the current significance of this area.

In this changing and unstable international system, both European and Asian partners of ASEM are facing challenges and great opportunities. Here I would like to discuss two projects that, though Chinese in origin, could benefit many ASEM countries and their respective societies: the New Silk Road and the Asian Infrastructure Investment Bank (AIIB).

The ongoing project of the New Silk Road between China and Europe is a novelty with potentially far-reaching consequences. Indeed a great physical integration is taking place between Central Asia and Europe. China has already invested in the New Silk Road a huge amount of dollars. And this huge amount of money is only the beginning of larger and larger financial investments. Like the ancient Silk Road, it will involve land and maritime routes.

The interest of China and Europe in the Silk Road is clear. With the European Union (EU) being China's biggest trading partner, a logistical route that improves economic integration between the Chinese industrial base and the

European one is not in need of a sophisticated explanation. With this transcontinental logistical project, China is also trying to develop industrial hubs in the interior of the country, which is an area with great economic potential and will likely be the future engine of growth. While trains now take less than two weeks to go from Chongqing in central China to Duisburg, with the new Silk Road, the journey time will be further reduced.

The new terrestrial link between Europe and China is not going to benefit only the "extremities" of the logistical route, but it is likely to have positive effects on the countries in between, some of which are also members of ASEM. Indeed, the new Silk Road will bring widespread regional benefits and will increase the importance of the lands between the two economic giants. Thus, many Asian states should maximize their unique geographical position. With the right strategy their position can be transformed into an economic and political asset.

The weak point of the new Silk Road is that any state between Europe and China can block the project. But since there are gains for everyone concerned, I believe that this opportunity will be exploited cooperatively. In case of emerging friction, ASEM is one of the key international fora in which to openly discuss and solve disputes. Accordingly, ASEM needs to invest its institutional capabilities and diplomatic skills in the new Silk Road and foster a cooperative environment not only between the EU and China, but especially with the countries situated between these two continental poles.

The newly created Chinese investment bank is another project with significant consequences for a number of Asian and European countries. The Asian Infrastructure Investment Bank, or AIIB, is an alternative both to the World Bank and to the Asian Development Bank (ADB). However, the Chinese-led bank is not simply a financial alternative to existing institutions. The AIIB, indeed, will employ more flexible and less exclusive criteria in its financing operations towards recipient countries than the ones currently used by the World Bank and the ADB. In particular, the AIIB will try to establish at the level of financial institutions the so-called "Beijing Consensus". But in order to be competitive with the World Bank and the ADB, the AIIB must create an efficient bureaucracy, managed according to high standards of governance. From this viewpoint, for China the AIIB is not merely an economic instrument with clear political goals, but it is also an intellectual and organisational challenge.

The membership of the new bank is also meaningful. A variety of developed countries such as Britain, Australia, France, Germany, and Italy joined the AIIB and many developing countries from all over the world have done the same, especially

ASEM members like India, Malaysia, the Philippines, Thailand, Viet Nam, and many others. Since infrastructure in some of these developing economies is greatly needed, the new financial institution is not only welcome, but it is an opportunity that must be capitalised. If long-term financing of major useful infrastructure projects takes off, rising economies might be strengthened and new poles of growth are likely to emerge.

In these new political and economic conditions, ASEM has the unique opportunity to contribute to a cooperative environment within Asia and between Europe and Asia, which is a key condition for peace and prosperity. Moreover, the success of ASEM will not be only an Asian and European success, but a positive development for international order and world economic growth. Let us, therefore, wish long life and success to ASEM.

Japan's Initiative for the Asia-Europe Meeting (ASEM)

by **Fumio KISHIDA**
Minister for Foreign Affairs
Japan

I n 2016, we will be celebrating the 20th Anniversary of the foundation of the Asia-Europe Meeting (ASEM), which started with its first summit meeting in Bangkok. Over the past two decades, Asia and Europe, which together account for around 60% of the global population, gross domestic product (GDP) and trade, have steadily deepened their relationship, both politically and economically. ASEM is a useful framework for conducting frank dialogue and further deepening cooperation with respect to issues of common interest for Asia and Europe.

For my part, I recently attended the 12th ASEM Foreign Ministers' Meeting (ASEM FMM12)[1] in Luxembourg to discuss with foreign ministers of other member states a wide range of issues, which include global issues such as climate

---

[1] www.aseminfoboard.org/events/12th-asem-foreign-ministers-meeting-asem-fmm12

change and development, responses to terrorism and extremism and the increasingly severe security environment in both Europe and Asia. Through this meeting, I once again recognised the roles played by Asia and Europe in promoting global peace and prosperity and renewed my resolve to strengthen our contributions to the two-decade-old ASEM process.

The fact that ASEM covers a wide range of themes, including politics, economy, society and culture, makes it possible to set timely agenda. Japan values ASEM as a forum that responds precisely and appropriately to the ever-changing international situation. Japan expects and hopes that ASEM will focus on political dialogue, connectivity and people-to-people exchanges in strengthening partnership between Europe and Asia, while maintaining these merits.

Political dialogue

ASEM is an important forum where heads of state and government and ministers from Asia and Europe get together to engage in frank exchanges of views about global challenges, such as terrorism, climate change, development and disaster management, as well as regional situations. The importance of political dialogue is growing, as the security environment in both Asia and Europe becomes increasingly severe year after year. The security of Asia and that of Europe are interconnected to each other, and it is very useful for political leaders from the two regions to hold candid discussions on how to ensure the peace and stability of the international community and to further deepen their common understanding and perspectives of this issue.

Above all, it is an important role of ASEM to ensure that Asia and Europe work together to maintain liberal and open international order by thoroughly upholding the principle of the "rule of law". In the Chair's Statement at the 10th ASEM Summit (ASEM10), ASEM made a reference to the principles of international law in the context of maritime security for the first time, and I highly appreciate this as something that has enhanced ASEM's significance.

Connectivity

When we think of ASEM's future, it is also important to achieve visible results by implementing more tangible cooperation. "Connectivity" is a comprehensive concept that not only concerns infrastructure but also applies to many other important areas, including trade, investment, education, culture and people-to-people exchanges. So we may say that connectivity, which is related to all of the three pillars of ASEM (politics, economy, culture & society), precisely embodies ASEM's activities.

As a field of connectivity, Japan is advocating the importance of tourism, which is the largest area of private sector exchanges and which can be expected to bring economic benefits. Tourism promotes mutual understanding through people-to-people and cultural exchanges and also accounts for 9% of global GDP. To promote tourism, environmental preservation as well as services, trade and investment are also important. In September 2015, Japan successfully hosted the ASEM Symposium on Promoting Tourism, which gathered participants from ASEM members, including ministers. Japan will continue efforts to promote tourism, including follow-up review of results, in cooperation with ASEM members.

At the same time, strengthening connectivity involves risk. As a result of increased cross-border connectivity, negative side effects - such as the spread of infectious diseases - may arise. Based on the understanding that taking countermeasures against possible pandemic outbreaks is part of important infrastructure development for strengthening connectivity, Japan is implementing the Project for the Rapid Containment of Pandemic Influenza[2] through cooperation with Asia-Europe Foundation (ASEF).

Furthermore, Japan believes it is necessary to devote efforts

---

[2]   ASEF Public Health Network, www. asef.org/projects/programmes/523-asef-public-health-network

to the fight against terrorism in consideration of the terrorist attacks in Paris in November 2015.

Strengthening people-to-people exchange

People-to-people connections form the heart of partnership between Asia and Europe. In particular, as Japan is convinced of the importance of exchanges between young people and students on whose shoulders the future of ASEM members rests, we have been striving to promote youth exchange. At the 1st ASEM Summit (ASEM1), Japan, together with Austria, proposed the Asia-Europe Young Leaders Symposium. This gathering, which was held every year between 1997 and 2008, brought together young leaders in various fields from Asia and Europe to discuss new ways of cooperation between the two regions. In addition, using funds contributed by Japan to ASEF, the Model ASEM was organised on the occasion of the 10th ASEM Summit (ASEM10) in 2014 and the ASEF Young Leaders Summit was held on the occasion of the 12th ASEM Foreign Ministers' Meeting (ASEM FMM12) in 2015. For ASEM's future, I believe that such activities and exchanges conducted by young people will play a significant role.

This year when we mark ASEM's 20th Anniversary at the Summit Meeting scheduled to be held in Ulaanbaatar (Mongolia) in July, I am sure it will be a milestone event in setting the future directions of ASEM based on the strengths and achievements accumulated over the past two decades. For its part, Japan is resolved to continue to place emphasis on ASEM's function as a framework for moderate dialogue and cooperation and to contribute to the ASEM process, in recognition of ASEM as an important forum for political dialogue, economic cooperation and cultural and social exchanges between Asia and Europe.

Building a Joint Future for ASEM: View from Kazakhstan

by **Erlan IDRISSOV**
Minister of Foreign Affairs
Republic of Kazakhstan

From its first days as an independent country, Kazakhstan has been guided by the principle of "economy first and then politics". Thanks to this principle and the leadership of President Nursultan NAZARBAYEV, our country has developed its economy very rapidly.

We are now determined to build on this success and, with the adoption of the "Kazakhstan - 2050" strategy, have set a goal of joining the list of the world's 30 most developed countries. With this strategy and by strengthening cooperation and dialogue with our international partners, we intend to develop our domestic industries, gain modern experience, attract innovations, exchange technologies and develop investment cooperation.

These are challenging times for the world. But Kazakhstan has enough resources to chart its way through the current international economic and political difficulties to continue improving the country's economy and the well-being of its citizens.

This resilience has been helped by policies to improve the investment climate which has seen Kazakhstan receive over US$100 billion in investment over the last five years.

It is impossible for any country to have a stable economy if it ignores what happens outside its borders. Kazakhstan, from its earliest days, has pursued policies to strengthen security and peace on the basis of international law and to be seen as a trusted partner.

We are an active participant in major international organisations such as the United Nations, Organization for Security and Cooperation in Europe, Organisation of Islamic Cooperation, Shanghai Cooperation Organization, and Conference on Interaction and Confidence Building Measures in Asia. We are committed to developing economic partnerships as well as strengthening our international relations.

Deepening economic cooperation is the aim of Kazakhstan's participation in the Eurasian Economic Union (EAEU) which started on 1 January, 2015. The EAEU is focused on building markets, broadening the transport-transit potential, and improving the social-economic environment. All this will be done within the framework of the World Trade Organization of which we became a member in 2015. We believe it will help us to expand our trade with the whole world and open new opportunities for our economy.

Our country is located where Asia and Europe meet. So it was natural for Kazakhstan to join the Asia-Europe Meeting (ASEM) which we did during the ASEM Summit in Milan in 2014.

There are many opportunities for increased cooperation. Our Development Strategy Kazakhstan 2050 and State Program "Nurly Zhol" (Path to the Future), for example, have been put in place to help us achieve the ambition of becoming one of the world's 30 most developed countries, and include policies designed to improve education and vocational training, energy efficiency technologies, transport and logistics, food security and energy innovations – all of which provide opportunities for new partnerships with ASEM members.

This is particularly the case in the transport and logistics spheres because of Kazakhstan's position as a bridge between Asia and Europe. A new railroad linking Kazakhstan, Turkmenistan and Iran that opens a shortcut to the Persian Gulf has been built, another new rail link connecting Almaty with Lianyungang port in China has been opened and a "Western Europe – Western China" road route nears completion. I strongly believe these improved transport links will help to strengthen cooperation with and between the ASEM countries.

The "Western Europe – Western China" road route is an example of the widespread benefits that Kazakhstan's improved transport infrastructure will bring. At present, the sea journey from China to Europe takes 24 days and the Trans-Siberia rail route 14 days. In contrast, transit on the new "Western Europe – Western China" route will take 10 days from Lianyungang to the borders of European countries.

Global climate change was one of the key topics at the meeting of ASEM Ministers of Foreign Affairs that was recently held in Luxembourg. Tackling this challenge will require all countries to change the way they power their economies. To help identify, develop and share the technologies that will be needed, our capital city, Astana, will host the International Exhibition "EXPO 2017" on the theme of "Future Energy". I am proud that many foreign countries and global companies have already confirmed their participation at this important event.

Ahead of EXPO 2017, Kazakhstan and the Asia-Europe Foundation (ASEF) have already held a seminar on "the problems of climate change in Central Asia and the development of the sphere of hydrocarbons" in April 2015. It was the first event that Kazakhstan had conducted with ASEM members and I am sure our cooperation will continue to be fruitful in the future.

The terrible danger that nuclear weapons pose to the world continues to be a major threat to all our safety and security. It is a threat that Kazakhstan knows well from its recent history: as a part of the Soviet Union, our country was the scene of 450 nuclear tests over 40 years and suffered badly. Even before Kazakhstan became formally independent, President NAZARBAYEV closed the Semipalatinsk nuclear testing site in 1991. Today Kazakhstan continues to work tirelessly in the international arena to end nuclear weapon tests, to halt the proliferation of weapons of mass destruction and to champion the cause of nuclear disarmament.

The ATOM project, which stands for "Abolish Testing, Our Mission", is an important part of this campaign. It is focused on raising awareness of the threat of nuclear weapons on humans and the environment all over the world.

Kazakhstan has also taken steps to help the expansion of peaceful nuclear power without increasing the dangers of the spread of nuclear weapons. Our country has agreed with the International Atomic Energy Agency to host the world's first Low-Enriched Uranium (LEU) Bank from 2017. It is an important step towards the strengthening of cooperation in the area of atomic energy and in establishing a safer world.

Kazakhstan is proud to have built a society in which people of many faiths and backgrounds live in harmony. In a world in which there are many religious, military and political conflicts, the need for tolerance and understanding is more important than ever. It was to build this understanding and respect that President NAZARBAYEV established the Congress of the Leaders of World and Traditional Religions that is held in our capital Astana every three years.

It is to help heal divisions, foster peace and cooperation, and build prosperity across the world that Kazakhstan is seeking a seat on the United Nations Security Council as a Non-Permanent Member for 2017-2018. I know these goals are also important to ASEM countries, and Kazakhstan looks forward to working to achieve these ambitions in close collaboration and coordination with the member states.

Kazakhstan's above mentioned initiatives such as EXPO 2017 and the LEU Bank were mentioned in the Chair's Statement of the ASEM Ministerial Meeting in Luxembourg. It shows that the world community members share the same goals with Kazakhstan in building a better world.

All this leads Kazakhstan to seek forging new humanitarian, socioeconomic and political links within the ASEM. We stand ready to further develop all relevant projects initiated by other members of this distinguished forum.

Connectivity as the Key Feature of ASEM's Third Decade

by **Jean ASSELBORN**
Minister for Foreign and European Affairs
Luxembourg

2016 is a critical year for Asia-Europe partnership as we prepare to celebrate the 20th Anniversary of Asia-Europe Meeting (ASEM) in Mongolia at the Ulaanbaatar Summit in July 2016, which will also mark the beginning of ASEM's third decade.

The 12th ASEM Foreign Ministers Meeting (ASEM FMM12) which I hosted in Luxembourg in 5-6 November, 2015 and which was chaired by the European Union's (EU) High Representative for Foreign Affairs and Security Policy, and Vice-President of the European Commission, Federica MOGHERINI, was a key event in discussing the future direction of ASEM and paving the way for its next decade.

Under the meeting theme "Working together for a sustainable and secure future", we reaffirmed that ASEM remained an important platform for political dialogue, economic cooperation as well as cultural and social exchanges between Asia and Europe. We also acknowledged the importance in mainstreaming connectivity into all relevant ASEM cooperation frameworks. We therefore agreed to further explore the establishment of a working group on connectivity as we commended the ever-growing activities on connectivity in the ASEM framework, which underline ASEM as an ideal platform for connecting Asia and Europe closer together.

ASEM as the "institutional home" to connectivity

Connectivity has so far mostly been dealt within regional organisations or at national levels. The EU for instance has established its border-free single market by providing a regulatory framework which seeks to guarantee the free movement of goods, capital, services and people between its member states. These efforts have recently been complemented by specific work on the digital single market, the energy union as well as a single market for financial services. Infrastructure-wise, the EU's single market has been enabled through the construction of the *Trans-European Networks*, a dense priority network of rail, road, energy and information and communications technology (ICT) infrastructure improving interconnection between the EU's 28 member states.

Similarly the 10 Association of Southeast Asian Nations (ASEAN) countries adopted in 2010 the "ASEAN Master Plan for Connectivity" which seeks to provide for enhanced physical infrastructure development (physical connectivity), effective institutions, mechanisms and processes (institutional connectivity) and empowered people (people-to-people connectivity) which have been considered as vital building blocks in the establishment of the ASEAN Community in November 2015.

For the rest of Asia, connectivity has so far mainly been on the agenda at the national level, as governments are trying to develop often basic infrastructure and to interconnect the various communities of large and populated countries. It was only two years ago that China's ambitious "One Belt, One Road" (OBOR) initiative had brought the item of interconnecting Asia and Europe onto the international agenda. However, the subject of "connectivity between Asia and Europe" has so far not been addressed by any international forum other than ASEM and thus has no "institutional home".

By bringing together representatives from all countries of Asia and Europe, ASEM is already a "connector platform" between Asia and Europe. In gathering expertise, know-how

and experience from both continents around a very concrete and tangible concept such as connectivity, ASEM can create specific added-value and wealth to both regions and their peoples.

The significance of Asia-Europe connectivity was stressed by the ASEM summit (ASEM10) in Milan in October 2014 with the Leaders underlining the contribution that increased ties could make to economic prosperity and sustainable development and to promoting free and seamless movement of people, trade, investment, energy, information, knowledge and ideas and greater institutional linkages. They noted the usefulness of an exchange of best practices and experiences. This was similarly reiterated and further discussed at the occasion of the 3rd ASEM Transport Ministers' Meeting (ASEM TMM3) in Riga, Latvia in April 2015 as well as at the ASEM Industry Dialogue on Connectivity in Chongqing, China in May 2015, which Luxembourg co-sponsored.

Setting the connectivity agenda in Ulaanbaatar

The challenge ahead of the 11th ASEM summit (ASEM11) in Ulaanbaatar is to turn our Leaders' words into policies and actions and at the same time to set the scope of the connectivity we all aim for. Recent conferences and meetings have tended to centre connectivity on obvious priorities: transport and infrastructure connectivity in order to build what transport ministers in Riga referred to as "the Eurasian multimodal transport corridors and supply chains". The meeting in Chongqing ambitiously referred to the improvement and building of new "Eurasian land bridges, Trans-Eurasian transport corridors", the upgrading of sea routes, high-speed rail links and work on an "information highway".

But in addition to upgrading road, sea and rail links our Leaders at the Milan summit in 2014 expressed an interest to examine ways of enhancing digital connectivity between Europe and Asia. This interest was further recalled at the ASEM FMM12 in Luxembourg when digital connectivity was highlighted as a key element of connecting our two regions. The Foreign Ministers also emphasised that greater collaboration among ASEM partners in the area of capacity building and exchange of expertise in ensuring security and peaceful development of ICT was essential.

The scope for a stronger digital connectivity remains therefore very high as our countries aim to develop further e-commerce and online trading opportunities, while a fair share of future communications will be satellite-based. Higher levels of digital connectivity will naturally contribute to bridging the digital divide and bringing our people closer to each other, the latter remaining one of the main goals of the ASEM process.

People-to-people connectivity

In 1996 in Bangkok at the 1st ASEM summit (ASEM1), 25 countries came together to promote the "new comprehensive Asia-Europe partnership for greater growth". And 20 years later, ASEM has more than doubled its membership and organised hundreds of meetings and seminars in areas such as education, human rights, transport, tourism, culture, research, immigration, disaster risk reduction, renewable energies, nuclear safety and youth employment. This reflects how ASEM as a framework for dialogue and cooperation has adapted and grown over the years to address the challenges and discuss the opportunities of our times. By way of example, Luxembourg hosted on the sidelines of the ASEM FMM12 in November 2015, two groups that held timely discussions on current and highly relevant issues. "Youth Employment" was the main topic at the first ASEF Young Leaders Summit[1], which successfully gathered over 100 young leaders from Asia and Europe. Additionally over 30 journalists from the two regions participated at the 10th ASEF Journalists' Colloquium[2] to exchange views on "Crisis Reporting".

---

[1] 1st ASEF Young Leaders' Summit, www.asef.org/projects/themes/education/3411-asef-young-leaders-summit-2015

[2] 10th ASEF Journalists' Colloquium, www.asef.org/projects/themes/sustainable-development/3412-10th-asef-journalists-colloquium

The success and the undeniable added-value of these events demonstrate that "people-to-people" connectivity needs to be rightly strengthened over the next decade by further involving the youth, universities, parliaments, research institutions and the private sector which will surely contribute to, enrich and expand the ASEM process.

The Economic and Social Significance of Creativity

by **Jet BUSSEMAKER**
Minister of Education, Culture and Science
the Netherlands

I n reflecting in this essay for the Asia-Europe Meeting (ASEM) 20th Anniversary publication, my mind inevitably went back to the 6th ASEM Culture Ministers' Meeting (ASEM CMM6)[1] held in 2014 in Rotterdam. That meeting showed that the creative industries could act as catalysts in enhancing the cultural cooperation between Asia and Europe. So, I am very pleased that the creative industries will also be on the main agenda for the next meeting of Culture Ministers in Gwangju, South Korea in 2016.

The Rotterdam meeting reinforced the conviction that our economies were becoming more cultural in nature and that the economic and social significance of creativity was growing.

The start of the 21st century has required Asia and Europe to

---

[1] www.aseminfoboard.org/events/6th-asem-culture-ministers-meeting-asem-cmm6

employ development strategies in order to foster human creative potential that can respond to the cultural, economic, social and technological shifts taking place. It was acknowledged that the creative industries have the ability to make use of culture to provide new insights and solutions to benefit both societal and economic goals.

At the same time, ASEM Culture Ministers acknowledged that many countries that have placed the creative industries on the policy agenda faced challenges. How to create links between different creative entrepreneurs and between entrepreneurs in creative and 'non-creative' sectors? How to broker opportunities for education and science to interact with the creative industries? And, how to make these developments reinforce initiatives at regional and city levels reciprocally?

The Ministers underlined that, in seeking answers to these questions, they had to recognise the value of the creative industries for creating a competitive advantage. Innovation does not come through technological advancement per se: technological advancement can also be traced back to imagination, creativity and craftsmanship.

Observations on creative industries

As this is a subject that is close to my heart, I would like to share some observations and guiding principles on government policy with regard to the creative industries.

The creative industry is characterised not only by innovative products and services with cultural and economic values, but also by its working methods.

A creative entrepreneur takes the needs of the consumer as a starting point and uses the power of imagination and prototyping to make the end result of a product tangible to the public even in the early phases of its development. That approach makes it possible for the creative industry to tackle complex issues and to come up with unexpected, innovative solutions using the latest technology available. That is one of the reasons why the market is looking at the creative industries to provide creative solutions for societal problems. I would like to mention, as an example, the Dutch clothing manufacturer G-STAR, which has developed a clothing line with the American singer-producer-designer, Pharrell WILLIAMS, wherein the clothes are made from plastic waste retrieved from the sea.

The dynamics of the creative industries have many advantages. By working in flexible, international and interdisciplinary networks, the sector is able to react very fast to the needs of the market. And, the growing number of start-ups provide for inventiveness and a continuous supply of innovative ideas.

However, the dynamics of the sector also carry a risk. For example, in a country like the Netherlands, the number of new companies has risen much more sharply than the number of people working in the creative industries. This downsizing in scale tends to lead to a loss in productivity as well as a loss in added value. As a result, the creative entrepreneur often lacks the time and the financial resources to develop a sustainable business model. This is compounded by the fact that traditional financial instruments are often not available to creative entrepreneurs.

In a policy paper that I recently submitted to the Parliament of the Netherlands, I identified a number of areas where government support could be instrumental for the creative industries.

Education

For an industry that relies on creativity, innovation is essential. That, in turn, calls for a strong emphasis on both personal development and permanent, lifelong learning. The creative industry as a whole needs to establish a tradition of combining business development with staff development through, among others, learning plans.

The demand for responsive and creative professionals requires that we look at our educational system. Our educational

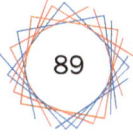

system needs to prepare us for the future. This, not only by providing the knowledge and skills that we currently know, but also by nurturing the capacity to develop new ways of thinking and the ability to adapt to new, at present unforeseen, changes in our environment. What does this mean for our educational system? How can we adjust our educational system such that it will stimulate students to develop their curiosity and creativity even more than it already does? How can our educational system help our citizens to break away from existing patterns of thinking and working?

When I look around me, I see both in the Netherlands and many other countries, promising signs that we are moving in the right direction. For example, in the fields of cultural and technology education, where teamwork, free expression, working with one's hands and a critical mindset have become important ingredients.

Craftsmanship

One area of the creative industries where, in my view, the educational approach deserves special attention is the field of creative craftsmanship.

Next to each designer stands a craftsman who can work side by side with the creative entrepreneur to develop his or her ideas and who is able to translate these ideas into practical solutions and products. Sometimes these craftsmen can be found abroad, but I think it is important to continue to train these craftsmen in one's own country and to treasure and safeguard traditional crafts that are still useful and relevant for the creative industry of today and the future.

Finance

One of the most common bottlenecks for a creative entrepreneur is the inability to invest in research. Most creative industries are too small and lack the financial means for research. At the same time, research - in many cases - is focused on long-term perspectives and on long-term results that do not fit the needs of the creative entrepreneur. To make it worthwhile and relevant for small- and medium-sized companies to participate in long-term research, governments, with the support of larger and financially strong companies, can help stimulate private-public research programmes that are tailor-made for the relatively smaller-sized creative industries.

I look forward to the discussion with my Asian and European colleagues on this subject at the upcoming ASEM Culture Ministers' Meeting (ASEM CMM7)[2] in Gwangju in 2016. And, I congratulate the Asia-Europe Foundation (ASEF) on the 20th Anniversary of the ASEM process.

---

[2] www.aseminfoboard.org/events/7th-asem-culture-ministers-meeting-asem-cmm7

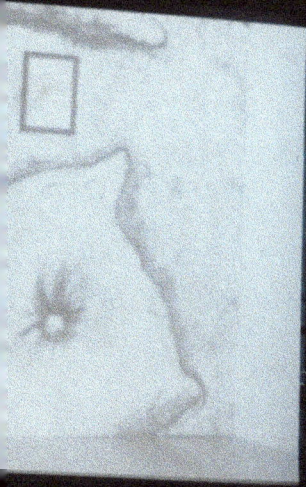

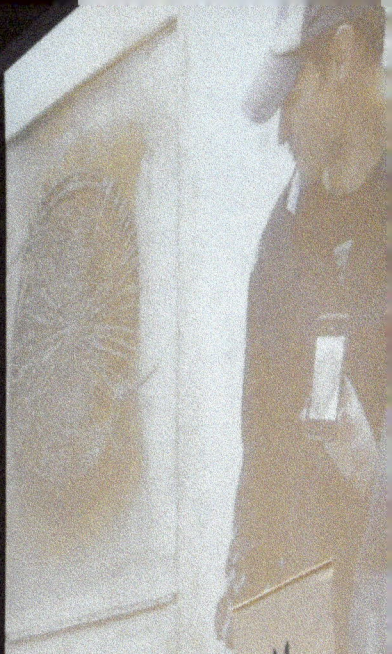

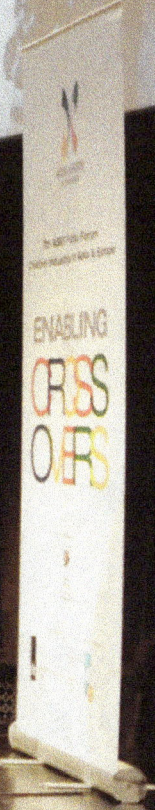

Role of Culture and the Arts for the Promotion of Mutual Understanding and Development between Asia and Europe

by **KIM Jongdeok**
Minister of Culture, Sports and Tourism
Republic of Korea

A s Minister of Culture, Sports and Tourism of the Republic of Korea, I am pleased to send heartfelt congratulations on the 20th Anniversary of the Asia-Europe Meeting (ASEM), a central forum for cooperation between the two regions. Cooperation requires unceasing efforts for mutual understanding, and for this reason, I am grateful to ASEM and the Asia-Europe Foundation (ASEF) for taking the principal initiative in promoting such efforts.

Underlying the recent tragic terror attacks in Paris and Brussels and all other conflicts is an absence of recognition of the necessity of working together for mutual understanding and growth. The 10th ASEM Summit (ASEM10) in Milan in

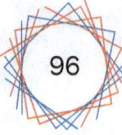

October 2014 discussed "Responsible Partnership for Growth and Security". It behooves us to continue to work hard to find measures to promote such a partnership to prevent any recurrence of tragic incidents.

As part of these international efforts, the Korean Government is doing what it can to the best of its ability to step up cooperation with ASEM and ASEF. The 8th ASEF Public Forum on Creative Cities in Asia and Europe[1] was held in Korea this year, and the 7th ASEM Culture Ministers' Meeting (ASEM CMM7) will also take place at the Asia Culture Center (ACC) in Gwangju in 2016. The ACC, which was opened to the public in October 2015, is Asia's largest culture and arts exchange organisation. The Center is expected to serve as a platform for interactions among Asian countries in culture and the arts and active exchanges with other parts of the world.

The Korean Government views communication anchored in a respect for the core values of culture as the essential foundation for viable cooperation and partnership activities based on mutual understanding. Accordingly, the Government is carrying out a nation branding campaign with a view to enhancing understanding of Korean core cultural values and, through this, is striving to seek new ways to promote

---

[1] 8th ASEF Public Forum, www.asef.org/projects/themes/culture/3469-ASEFPublicForum8

cooperation and communication with countries around the world.

As part of its endeavours to explore core cultural values, the Korean Government is concentrating on tapping into the potential of traditional culture. Despite the acceleration of globalisation, traditional culture remains as the intrinsic element of every country's identity. As declared by United Nations Educational, Scientific and Cultural Organization (UNESCO), preservation and exchanges of traditional culture will play a pivotal role in protecting and promoting the diversity of cultural expression in the international community. For years, the Korean Wave, particularly of such pop culture as K-pop, films and dramas, has reached many parts of the world. In the wake of the spread of the Korean Wave, the Korean Government is now planning on actively implementing policies for mutual exchanges aimed at promoting Korean traditional culture around the world and introducing Asian and European cultures to Koreans.

As demonstrated by the theme of the 7th ASEM Culture Ministers' Meeting (ASEM CMM7), "Culture and Creative Economy", the concept of a creative economy is being seriously considered by many countries around the world in a variety of areas beyond the economy, including the arts, culture and social affairs. In addition to the value of arts and culture as creative activities, Korea is also paying keen attention to their potential value to the economy and industries. Believing that the creative economy initiative will become a new engine for economic growth, the Korean Government is planning to make sustained investments in the cultural content industry. Among other things, the Cultural Creation Convergence Belt, which is being created to serve as a platform that helps facilitate the overall process of planning, production, distribution and enjoyment of cultural content, will play a leading role in further promoting the production of cultural content and distribution at home and abroad. It will also serve as the main pillar for cooperation in the creative economy. On top of this, the Korean Government is striving to make thorough preparations for the PyeongChang 2018 Winter Olympics so that culture, tourism, content and information and communications technology (ICT) all combine harmoniously to promote mutual understanding and meaningful interaction among participants from about 100 countries.

Since its establishment, ASEM has discussed pending issues and risks with the international community and set directions for mutual understanding and cooperation. Now there needs to be full, continued dialogue, through which we can come up with concrete solutions for mutual progress in both Asia and Europe. We also need to contemplate the best way to achieve diverse, multilateral exchanges and cooperation beyond the two continents and establish a framework to carry them out.

As an ASEM member state, the Korean Government stands fully committed to seeking ways to promote the mutual development of Asia and Europe. It will fully support such a process with a firm belief that working together with ASEM will lead to an invaluable journey to the future.

Again, my heartfelt congratulations and gratitude on the 20th Anniversary of ASEM.

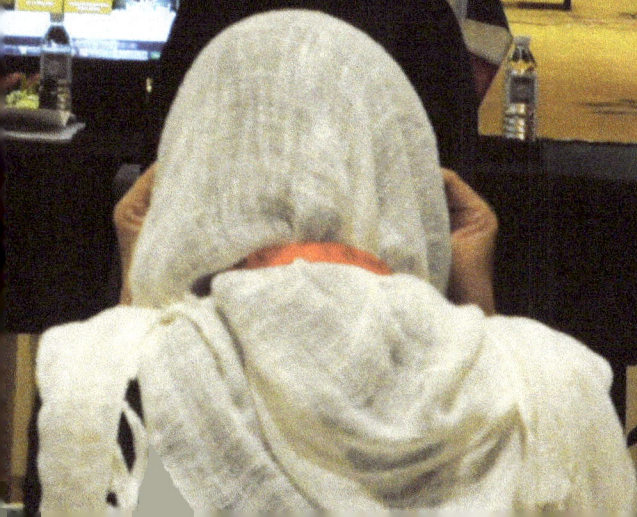

Sweden's Contribution to the ASEM Informal Seminars on Human Rights

by **Margot WALLSTRÖM**
Minister for Foreign Affairs
Sweden

L aunched in 1997 by Sweden and France, the Asia-Europe
Meeting (ASEM) Informal Seminar on Human Rights[1]
has become one of the longest lasting components
of ASEM Tangible Cooperation. Co-organised with the
Philippines, the 15th edition of the seminar recently took place
in Montreux, Switzerland, on the theme of "Human Rights
and Trafficking in Persons".

The very 1st ASEM Informal Seminar on Human Rights
was held at the Raoul Wallenberg Institute at the University of
Lund in southern Sweden. The theme of that inaugural seminar
was "Human Rights and the Rule of Law: Administration of
Justice".

---

[1] www.asef.org/projects/programmes/533-informal-asem-seminar-on-human-rights

Back in 1997, the 1993 Vienna Declaration and Programme of Action adopted by the World Conference on Human Rights were fresh in the minds of the participants. It seemed that the road was open for an ever stronger focus on how human rights and the rule of law could be improved all over the world.

And much has indeed generally improved in the world since then. More countries have formally adopted democracy. The total number of executions worldwide has declined. Women increasingly participate in decision-making. More children go to school and people have access to better medical care. The number of people living in absolute poverty is decreasing. These are major steps forward.

But looking around at this particular juncture, the world has again become more unpredictable and less secure. In 2015, for the ninth consecutive year, several countries have again experienced a deterioration of democracy and human rights. Authoritarian and repressive regimes are gaining influence, both over their own citizens and worldwide. Terrorist groups commit atrocities in areas devoid of civilisation. Democratic space is shrinking. The possibilities for civil society to contribute to better development are being reduced, freedom of expression is being curtailed and universal rights are being questioned.

We need to continue to try to broaden democratic space. As human rights are being challenged, voices of freedom silenced by imprisonment and the rule of law flagrantly flouted and obstructed, we need to work even more diligently to defend freedom of expression and ensure the means for civil society to exist and work. Right now, disinformation and propaganda have put an entire generation at risk of being unable to form their own views about society and the world around them.

The rule of law is essential to fight corruption. However, corruption is eating into and undermining the rule of law. The consequences are serious when holding a public office becomes a means of obtaining illicit material gains. The ability of societies to carry out political intentions is weakened. Corruption also leads to transnational crime and reduces our security.

In order to live up to the rule of law and true democracy, it is essential that women and girls are able to enjoy their human rights. The involvement of women is imperative to ensure peace and security. Societies with gender balance run less risk of violence and conflict. For these reasons, Sweden now has a feminist foreign policy. We believe that the empowerment of women and girls is a prerequisite for an economically, socially and environmentally sustainable world.

Much remains to be done when it comes to strengthening economic and social rights. The global goals established in the new 2030 Agenda for Development by all members of the United Nations are great steps forward. Implementing the 2030

Agenda will be crucial to fulfilling many of these rights.

In this context, both states and private sector companies have responsibilities regarding decent working conditions and the right to organise in labour unions. People's voices need to be heard in relation to the distribution of land resources and agricultural land.

Establishing and supporting fora where people from different countries and continents can meet and freely discuss issues is vital to our ability to work towards a better understanding of all aspects of human rights. The Asia-Europe Foundation (ASEF) provides important platforms that enable such free-flowing discussions.

The ASEM Informal Seminar on Human Rights will continue to be a forum where governments, academia and civil society can meet and discuss issues of common concern to all of mankind. Later this year, China will host the seminar on the theme of Human Rights and Persons with Disabilities. We look forward to interesting and in-depth discussions on this very timely topic which is of great concern to all of us.

Countering all forms of discrimination and violence based on ethnicity, religion, gender, sexual orientation or disability is vital. We can now see that continued discrimination against lesbian, gay, bisexual and transgender (LGBT) persons remains

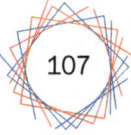

one of the great challenges of our time and needs to be addressed
– perhaps in a future ASEM Seminar on Human Rights.

24-26 November 2015
Montreux, Switzerland
www.aseminfoboard.org

Human Rights and Trafficking in Persons
15th Informal ASEM Seminar on Human Rights

ASEM AND ASEF

Reflections on ASEF

by **Tommy KOH**
Ambassador-At-Large
Ministry of Foreign Affairs
Singapore

and **Peggy KEK**
Former Director of Public Affairs
Asia-Europe Foundation (ASEF)

Introduction

The establishment of the Asia-Europe Foundation (ASEF), under the auspices of Asia-Europe Meeting (ASEM) was a significant and concrete contribution to people-to-people relations between Asia and Europe.

At a meeting of senior officials in Dublin in December 1996, ASEM members adopted by consensus the so-called Dublin Principles that would form the foundation of ASEF. Singapore offered to host the Foundation and a year after the first ASEM took place in Bangkok, ASEF was launched in the republic in February 1997, by the 26 founding members of ASEM.

ASEF's first home was a gracious black and white bungalow with extensive grounds at No. 1 Nassim Hill, within walking distance of the Singapore Botanic Gardens. As we were the founding Executive Director and Director of Public Affairs respectively, we had the great pleasure of working in that beautiful office from 1997 to 2000.

Unique mandate

We found those three years exhilarating. There was much to be done, and much that could be done. As far as we could tell, there was no other organisation in the world like ASEF.

While there are other organisations that aim to promote understanding between countries, they mostly do so on behalf of only one country, albeit reaching out to many others. Examples of these are the Alliance Française, British Council, Goethe Institute, Confucius Institute, Instituto Cervantes, Istituto Italiano di Cultura, and Nehru Centre.

Although the Commonwealth institutions seek in some way to promote understanding among multiple countries, the member countries all share a common history of having been part of the British Empire and share the same language.

On the other hand, ASEM membership was based on a shared vision, born in Bangkok, to reconnect two important regions and civilisations of the world. Initially, the membership was confined to the European Union, Association of Southeast Asian Nations (ASEAN) and three states of Northeast Asia, namely, China, Japan and South Korea.

Sense of ownership

As members of the start-up team, we had the challenge and the opportunity to introduce ASEF to the world. We had to convince institutions in ASEM member countries to work with us. To them, ASEF was an unknown quantity. To succeed, we knew that we would need the support of enthusiastic and loyal champions. We were fortunate that we had some early believers, who, in turn, helped us to win over more supporters.

We needed to raise the profile of ASEF quickly, encourage participation in our projects and events, and give ASEM members a sense of ownership of ASEF.

This last challenge was particularly difficult as ASEF had a physical presence only at the house on Nassim Hill. We avoided the easy option of holding all the projects in Singapore and instead worked extra hard to find relevant and willing partners in as many different countries and to involve participants from as many member countries as possible.

We were greatly helped by a supportive board, which trusted and provided useful advice to the management team. Prof Helmut HAUSSMANN, who has been the ASEF Governor for Germany since 1997, was instrumental in opening doors to German parliamentarians, think-tanks and foundations. The late Mr Edmond ISRAEL ensured that we had a direct line to the political leadership of Luxembourg. The late Ambassador Jay-Hee OH played a critical role in the success of ASEF's work at ASEM2, in Seoul, in October 2000.

We partnered organisations that had more established reputations and networks. In these respects, it greatly helped that Singapore was both an important destination for the world's political and business leaders and that Singaporean institutions were part of many international networks. When the Asian Financial Crisis occurred in 1998, it was felt in many of the affected Asian countries that the crisis had been misunderstood by the Western countries and institutions including the International Monetary Fund (IMF). So, taking advantage of the pulling power of the World Economic Forum (WEF) and the presence of Europe's media in Singapore for the WEF East Asia Summit, ASEF initiated a Colloquium for Journalists for a discussion on how Europe could help Asia without creating a backlash.

With the help of INSEAD, we were able to organise, at their Fontainebleau campus in France, a conference to discuss the idea of an Asia-Europe Education Hub. With that, a new network of Asian and European universities was launched.

Building bridges and networks

We set about our mission by being a creator of new networks, an interpreter of key developments and events, and an intellectual bridge-builder. Our strategy included making sure that the projects we organised were relevant and newsworthy. In all these efforts, institutions and individuals from think tanks, the arts and cultural sector, and the media were our earliest supporters.

We created new Asia-Europe networks of arts groups, museums, parliamentarians, school students, universities, journalists and researchers. Many of these networks have continued to thrive with the support of subsequent ASEF management teams.

We also initiated projects that helped to explain significant developments in both regions such as the advent of the Euro and Indonesia's first democratic elections in 1999. For the latter, ASEF created a platform to help Europe better understand the historic event taking place in the most populous nation in Southeast Asia. We assembled a panel comprising representatives from all the major parties and invited journalists from all the ASEM countries to attend the Colloquium in Jakarta.

As an intellectual bridge-builder, we convened discussions on issues that often divided politicians and intellectuals of Asia and Europe - issues such as human rights and the question of Myanmar (also known as Burma). We also organised a seminar in Paris, with the support of the French Ministry of Finance, to discuss the causes of the Asian financial crisis and the prospects of Asia post-crisis.

Early challenges and champions

Singapore, France and Luxembourg were among the early champions of ASEF. The three countries made substantial financial contributions to help ASEF get off to a good start. In addition, France also seconded Pierre BARROUX as the Deputy Executive Director of ASEF.

In 1999, when Europeans were getting ready to launch the Euro, ASEF initiated a roadshow to provide Europe with a platform to introduce the Euro to Asia. We took the roadshow to Hong Kong, Beijing and Singapore with Jean-Claude TRICHET, Christian NOYER and Dominique STRAUSS-KAHN. This project could not have succeeded without the strong support of the government of France.

Luxembourg hosted the first Asia-Europe Editors Meeting in October 1997. The meeting was a wonderful platform to present ASEF to some 30 members of the media of Asia and Europe. Some of the editors we met at that first meeting became some of ASEF's most ardent supporters. Among them were the late Mr Felix SOH of Singapore's *Straits Times*, Mr Larry JAGAN, the founding editor of BBC World Service's East Asia

Today programme, Ms Shada ISLAM, formerly with the *Far Eastern Economic Review*, Mr Matthias NASS, the Editor of *Die Zeit* (Hamburg), Kavi CHONGKITTAVORN of *The Nation* (Bangkok), and Ambassador Sabam SIAGIAN, the publisher of the *Jakarta Post*. Many have remained great friends and supporters of ASEF and we were happy to learn that subsequent teams of ASEF have continued to maintain relations with this informal network.

Enduring flagship ASEF projects

Despite the changes in ASEM membership and ASEF management teams, some projects that were launched in the initial years of ASEF have not only survived over the years, but are in fact flourishing.

The ASEF Editors' Roundtable is now a mainstay event organised biennially on the sidelines of every ASEM Summit. The ASEF Journalists' Colloquium continues to bring the media together for significant developments and now has a regular scheduled spot on the sidelines of the ASEM Foreign Ministers' Meeting.

The ASEF Classroom Network (ASEF ClassNet) continues to foster collaboration among secondary and high school teachers and students in Asia and Europe. The ASEM Education Hub is now known as the ASEF

Higher Education Programme, and has given birth to four sub-programmes: ASEM Rectors' Conference and Students' Forum (ARC), Asia-Europe Education Workshops, ASEM Education and Research Hub for Lifelong Learning (ASEM LLL Hub), and the Database on Education Exchange Programmes (DEEP).

The ASEM Museum Network continues to thrive. The ASEM Informal Seminar on Human Rights continues to bring government officials, academics and civil society representatives from Asia and Europe for dialogues on difficult issues.

Major changes since 2000

ASEF has undergone many changes since 2000, when we stepped down. With these changes, there have been new opportunities and challenges.

One of the biggest changes is the number of ASEM members. From 26 members in 1997, ASEM now has 53 partners. This development alone has had significant implications on the way ASEF operates. As the founding principles had a provision for every ASEM member to be represented on the ASEF Board of Governors, this has made ASEF board meetings a much bigger undertaking now, both logistically and in agenda-setting.

On the positive side, this expansion means that there are,

potentially, many more sources of support, both intellectual and financial. It also means that there are more countries to reach out to, more countries in which to raise the profile of ASEF, and more countries among which to spread the projects. This also makes it much harder for ASEF to gain traction in each specific country.

Despite all the challenges it faces, ASEF continues to grow from strength to strength. The current management team has identified new areas of focus that are relevant to today's world. Two of the new themes to have emerged are public health and sustainable development.

Conclusion

Over the years, many nationals from ASEM member countries have served and continue to serve on the Board of Governors, management team and staff of ASEF. Today, 19 years after its establishment, ASEF remains the only brick and mortar institution of ASEM. It has played a unique and significant role in enhancing mutual understanding between Asia and Europe.

If ASEM members believe in the mission of ASEF, we sincerely hope that they will demonstrate this by making substantial and regular financial contributions to sustain the Foundation. After all, every ASEM member has a representative on the ASEF board, a say in the direction and work plan of ASEF, and therefore the responsibility to help ASEF thrive and succeed.

We hope the governments and peoples of ASEM countries will continue to uphold and provide staunch support for the mission of ASEF, and for the aspirations of ASEM, to build strong and meaningful multilateral relations between Asia and Europe.

About the Editor

Peggy KEK is a Singaporean. She was a member of the founding management team of the Asia-Europe Foundation (ASEF), serving as its first Director of Public Affairs from 1997 to 2000. Together with the former Executive Director, Ambassador Tommy Koh, she is honoured to have played a role in introducing ASEF to the world, establishing new institutional links and cooperation frameworks with ASEM partners. In the course of her three years with ASEF, she visited and worked with institutions in almost every one of the original partner countries. She fervently believes in the power and importance of partnerships to achieve greater public good, and has worked on building collaborative relationships throughout her career, which included roles at other international organisations namely, UNICEF, The World Bank (Washington DC) and The Asia Foundation. At home, she worked with the Singapore International Foundation, National University of Singapore and the Institute of Policy Studies (Singapore). Educated in Singapore and the United Kingdom, she speaks French and Chinese in addition to her native English, and is delighted to play a role again in building bridges between Asia and Europe, as the Editor of this book. She is the editor of *ASEF: Connecting Asia and Europe 1997-2000* (Singapore: Asia Europe Foundation, 2000), *A World of Ideas: Fifteen Years of the Institute* *of Policy Studies* (Singapore: Institute of Policy Studies, 2003), *Gotong Royong: Fifteen Years of Friendship with Indonesia* (Singapore: Singapore International Foundation, 2007) and most recently, *Singapore and UNICEF: Working for Children* (Singapore: World Scientific, January 2016).

About the Series

This special series of articles by the Asia-Europe Foundation (ASEF) is dedicated to the 20th Anniversary of the Asia-Europe Meeting (ASEM). The book will be distributed at the 11th Asia-Europe Meeting (ASEM11) Summit in 2016 in Mongolia. The articles have appeared in the ASEF eNewsletter and are also available on the ASEF website at **www.asef.org**